21 Poems

Lucy Finch

BookLeaf Publishing

Presentation by *BookLeaf Publishing*

Web: www.bookleafpub.com

E-mail: info@bookleafpub.com

ISBN: 9789357213820

First edition 2023

Number One

Poem number one
I could sing you a song
About all the things that have gone wrong
But instead
Sat snug in my bed
I will paint you the picture of a mouse with a
gong
He scurries from his hole
Cheese wedged in a bowl
To announce to all his friends
That dinner is served
A meal thoroughly deserved
For his whiskery friends of so long

Number Two

My former number two
I am thinking of you
But I must put you out of my mind
For after all
That pain won't help at all
And to myself I shan't be unkind
In lieu of this
I will think of the mist
On a moody dark overcast day
Although that seems sad
I'm just ever so glad
Unlike you, the fog will probably stay

Number Three

Poem number three
About the branches of a tree
A blackened beacon of good
I knelt by the charred
remains of the bard
Who once whispered dark tales to the wood
There was a fire inside
This tree when it died
A smouldering force of woe
Although gone are the branches
The there's a world of second chances
In the slumbering roots below

Number Four

When out walking at four
I found a small door
Carved into an old tree stump
I gave it a knock
Heard the sound of a lock
Then out came a rather cross Grump
A small little fellow
Short and stout
He wondered what the knocking was all about
I was taken aback
But I smiled with the knack
of someone well versed in the fae
I said forgive me dear sir
I am your new chauffeur
So he hopped in my bag for the day

Number Five

Keep counting to five
I've got to stay alive
This desert will claim me soon
I thought I was alright
Until the bewildering sight
Of that dish with his best pal the spoon

Number Six

6

Poem number six
It's a bit of a mix
Of horror and romance
I went to a ball
An exquisite hall
To join in the skeleton dance
Dressed in pure white
I gawked at the sight
Of silk and lace draped over bones
They moved with a clatter
Whilst a wolf served a platter
Of full-fat milk and scones

Number Seven

Poem number seven
The easy rhyme is heaven
I really did try
But my well has run dry
This one's no intellectual leaven

Number Eight

8

Number eight
Adorned on a gate
I venture inside on a whim
The garden is a mess
Thorns tug at my dress
The daylight has turned quite dim..

Number Nine

I catch the train at nine
The weather ain't too fine
There's a body on the track
I think he's broke his back
I hope I get to work on time

Number Ten

10

Watching the news at ten
From behind the sofa
Like we used to watch that Sci-Fi show

Number Eleven

When I was eleven
I was gifted a toy puppy for my birthday
I recall vividly
This final feeling
Of pure unadulterated joy

Number Twelve

12

When I was twelve
The depression started to haunt me
I could feel its malevolence creeping in
Making me feel things I didn't understand
Feeding off my friendships
Discarding them when it was done
To know now it had a name
Like a vicious dog
Does not bring back the years I've lost

Number Thirteen

Conversations with my thirteen year old self
A song I listened to on repeat
I fancied I could live life alone on the street
Free from boundaries
Free from the burden of love
As if I didn't need warmth
As if my young mind could be my only friend
I'm glad I never tried
I never ran away
I found a home in myself in the end

Number Fourteen

14

At age fourteen I liked a girl
I did not say a thing
She liked me back I found out later
Too late for my heart to sing

Number Fifteen

At fifteen I didn't have the sense
to tell a boy no in maths
But we were told to make choices
With uncertain young voices
That would narrow our winding paths
A worn walked track
that twelve years on
Is so overgrown with weeds
But I have learned to nurture them
And watch them bloom
Into flowers from ruin not seeds

Number Sixteen

16

Sixteen
Sick teen
Never was a prom queen
Summer days
Young love's gaze
So faint it's like a dream

Number Seventeen

At seventeen I learned the truth
Sitting in a theatre booth
When I was seventeen
I drank my very first beer
Before I'd felt the pressure of fear
On the edge of seventeen
I felt no doubt
But I didn't know yet what those songs were
about

Number Eighteen

At eighteen the world lay down at my feet
I danced and sang and swayed to the beat
If this year had a taste
It'd be cherry flavoured cola
A common flavour
Just a little more sweet

Number Nineteen

Nineteen was the year that changed it all
No more education
No more procrastination
I made my first true choices
As an adult woman
I paved the way for how my my life is now
That young girl took bold risks
Now this old girl can be here
Sitting in bed writing poems
Alive and with a future
She carved all by herself
At nineteen
The year that changed it all

Number Twenty

How is the Grump faring, you wonder
we're firm friends since my knocking blunder
Inside the fairy ring
Of twenty mushrooms - he is king
He rules the sky, the rain and the thunder

Number Twenty One

Poem twenty one
If you're still here and haven't gone
I wish you the best
You'll take care of the rest
Choose good ground for your life to grow on